50 Premium Egyptian Recipes

By: Kelly Johnson

Table of Contents

- Koshari (Egyptian Rice, Lentils, and Pasta)
- Molokhia (Jute Leaf Stew)
- Fattah (Rice, Meat, and Vinegar Sauce)
- Mahshi (Stuffed Vegetables)
- Shawarma (Egyptian-style Grilled Meat)
- Taameya (Egyptian Falafel)
- Kofta (Spiced Ground Meat Kebabs)
- Feseekh (Fermented Fish)
- Hamam Mahshi (Stuffed Pigeon)
- Roz Bel Laban (Rice Pudding)
- Moussaka (Eggplant and Ground Meat Casserole)
- Baba Ganoush (Eggplant Dip)
- Egyptian Tabbouleh
- Shorbat Adas (Lentil Soup)
- Mulukhiyah Soup with Chicken
- Sweets of Basbousa (Semolina Cake)
- Konafa (Shredded Phyllo Pastry with Syrup)

- Sahlab (Egyptian Orchid Drink)
- Samak Mashwi (Grilled Fish)
- Kebab Hala (Grilled Lamb Kebabs)
- Dukkah (Spice and Nut Mix)
- Eish Baladi (Egyptian Flatbread)
- Sayadeya (Fish Pilaf)
- Kebda Eskandarani (Alexandrian-style Liver)
- Warak Enab (Stuffed Grape Leaves)
- Shakshuka (Poached Eggs in Tomato Sauce)
- Sabich (Eggplant and Egg Sandwich)
- Chicken Mahshi (Stuffed Chicken)
- Shawarma Spiced Fries
- Batata Harra (Spicy Potatoes)
- Egyptian Koshari with Meat
- Tamarind Drink (Amr El-Din)
- Qatayef (Stuffed Pancakes)
- Shamsiya (Fried Pastry with Honey)
- Molokhia with Rabbit
- Bamia (Okra Stew)

- Hummus Bi Tahini (Chickpea Dip)
- Lentil and Rice Salad with Lemon Dressing
- Tzatziki-style Yogurt with Garlic and Cucumber
- Nile Perch with Tahini Sauce
- Sweet Potato and Honey Fritters
- Mashed Fava Beans (Ful Medames)
- Egyptian Falafel Sandwich
- Eish Meshmesh (Peach Bread)
- Beid Bel Daqa (Eggs with Spices)
- Sogok (Honeyed Pistachio Dessert)
- Al-Mahshi Kousa (Stuffed Zucchini)
- Smoked Salmon with Tahini
- Hawaij (Spiced Rice)
- Egyptian Pudding with Cinnamon (Om Ali)

Koshari (Egyptian Rice, Lentils, and Pasta)

Ingredients:

- 1 cup rice
- 1/2 cup brown lentils
- 1/2 cup elbow macaroni or spaghetti
- 1 onion, thinly sliced
- 2 tbsp olive oil
- 2 cloves garlic, minced
- 1 can (14 oz) crushed tomatoes
- 1 tbsp vinegar
- Salt and pepper

Instructions:

1. Cook lentils in water for about 20 minutes until tender.
2. Cook rice according to package instructions.
3. Cook pasta in salted water until al dente, then drain.
4. In a pan, sauté onions in olive oil until golden. Remove half for garnish.
5. Add garlic to the remaining onions, sauté for 1 minute, then add crushed tomatoes, vinegar, salt, and pepper. Simmer for 10 minutes.
6. To serve, layer rice, lentils, pasta, and top with tomato sauce. Garnish with crispy onions.

Molokhia (Jute Leaf Stew)

Ingredients:

- 1 lb molokhia (jute leaves), fresh or frozen
- 1 onion, chopped
- 4 cloves garlic, minced
- 4 cups chicken broth
- 2 tbsp butter
- 1 tsp cumin
- Salt and pepper
- Lemon wedges (for serving)
- Cooked rice (for serving)

Instructions:

1. In a pot, heat butter and sauté onions and garlic until fragrant.
2. Add molokhia leaves and chicken broth. Bring to a simmer and cook for 15-20 minutes.
3. Season with cumin, salt, and pepper.
4. Serve the stew over rice with a wedge of lemon on the side.

Fattah (Rice, Meat, and Vinegar Sauce)

Ingredients:

- 2 cups rice
- 1 lb beef or lamb, cut into cubes
- 1 onion, chopped
- 2 garlic cloves, minced
- 1 tsp cumin
- 1/2 cup vinegar
- 1/2 cup tomato sauce
- 1 cup chicken broth
- 2 tbsp ghee or butter
- Salt and pepper

Instructions:

1. Cook rice according to package instructions.
2. Brown meat in a pot, then add onions and garlic, cooking until soft.
3. Add cumin, tomato sauce, chicken broth, and vinegar. Simmer for 30 minutes until meat is tender.
4. In a separate pan, heat ghee or butter and fry some bread cubes until crispy.
5. To serve, layer the rice, top with meat and sauce, and garnish with crispy bread.

Mahshi (Stuffed Vegetables)

Ingredients:

- 4 zucchinis, hollowed out
- 4 bell peppers, hollowed out
- 4 tomatoes, hollowed out
- 1 cup rice, rinsed
- 1/2 lb ground beef or lamb
- 1 onion, chopped
- 1 tbsp tomato paste
- 1 tsp cinnamon
- 2 tsp dried mint
- Salt and pepper
- Olive oil
- 2 cups vegetable broth

Instructions:

1. Mix rice, ground meat, onions, tomato paste, cinnamon, mint, salt, and pepper.
2. Stuff vegetables with the mixture, securing with toothpicks.
3. Heat olive oil in a pot, then arrange stuffed vegetables in the pot.
4. Add vegetable broth, cover, and simmer for 40-45 minutes until vegetables are tender.

Shawarma (Egyptian-style Grilled Meat)

Ingredients:

- 1 lb chicken or beef, thinly sliced
- 3 tbsp olive oil
- 3 cloves garlic, minced
- 1 tbsp cumin
- 1 tbsp paprika
- 1 tbsp ground coriander
- 1 tsp turmeric
- 1/2 tsp cinnamon
- Juice of 1 lemon
- Salt and pepper
- Pita bread (for serving)
- Tahini or garlic sauce (for serving)

Instructions:

1. Mix olive oil, garlic, cumin, paprika, coriander, turmeric, cinnamon, lemon juice, salt, and pepper in a bowl.
2. Marinate meat in the spice mixture for at least 2 hours.
3. Grill or cook the meat in a hot pan for 5–7 minutes until cooked through.
4. Serve in pita bread with tahini or garlic sauce.

Taameya (Egyptian Falafel)

Ingredients:

- 2 cups dried fava beans, soaked overnight
- 1 onion, chopped
- 2 garlic cloves, minced
- 1 bunch parsley
- 1 bunch cilantro
- 1 tsp cumin
- 1 tsp coriander
- Salt and pepper
- Baking powder
- Oil for frying

Instructions:

1. Drain and rinse soaked fava beans.
2. Combine beans, onion, garlic, parsley, cilantro, cumin, coriander, salt, and pepper in a food processor.
3. Add baking powder and form into small patties.
4. Heat oil in a pan and fry patties until golden brown, about 4-5 minutes per side.
5. Serve with pita bread and tahini sauce.

Kofta (Spiced Ground Meat Kebabs)

Ingredients:

- 1 lb ground beef or lamb
- 1 onion, finely chopped
- 1/4 cup parsley, chopped
- 1 tsp cumin
- 1 tsp paprika
- Salt and pepper
- Wooden skewers (soaked in water)

Instructions:

1. Mix ground meat with onion, parsley, cumin, paprika, salt, and pepper.
2. Form mixture into long kebabs around the skewers.
3. Grill or broil the kofta for 10–12 minutes, turning occasionally.
4. Serve with rice or flatbread.

Feseekh (Fermented Fish)

Ingredients:

- 1 whole fish (typically mullet), salted and fermented
- Olive oil
- Lemons, for squeezing
- Onion, for garnish

Instructions:

1. Clean the fermented fish and remove bones if desired.
2. Serve with olive oil, lemon wedges, and onion slices.
3. Typically enjoyed with flatbread.

Hamam Mahshi (Stuffed Pigeon)

Ingredients:

- 4 pigeons (or Cornish hens as an alternative)
- 1 cup rice, rinsed
- 1/2 lb ground beef or lamb
- 1 onion, finely chopped
- 2 tbsp pine nuts
- 2 tbsp butter
- 1 tsp cinnamon
- 1 tsp allspice
- Salt and pepper
- 2 cups chicken or vegetable broth
- 2 tbsp ghee (optional)

Instructions:

1. Cook rice with some butter and spices (cinnamon, allspice) until tender.
2. In a pan, sauté onions and pine nuts until golden, then add the ground meat and cook through.
3. Mix the cooked rice and meat together and stuff the pigeons.
4. Place stuffed pigeons in a pot, cover with broth, and cook over low heat for 45–60 minutes until tender.

5. Optionally, brown the stuffed pigeons in a hot pan with ghee before serving.

Roz Bel Laban (Rice Pudding)

Ingredients:

- 1/2 cup short-grain rice
- 4 cups milk
- 1/2 cup sugar
- 1 tsp vanilla extract
- 1 tbsp cornstarch (optional for extra creaminess)
- Ground cinnamon for garnish (optional)

Instructions:

1. Rinse rice under cold water.
2. In a saucepan, bring milk and rice to a simmer. Cook for 30 minutes, stirring often until the rice is tender.
3. Add sugar and continue cooking for 10 minutes.
4. Stir in vanilla extract. If you want a thicker consistency, mix cornstarch with a little milk and add it to the pudding.
5. Serve warm or chilled with a sprinkle of cinnamon.

Moussaka (Eggplant and Ground Meat Casserole)

Ingredients:

- 2 large eggplants, sliced
- 1 lb ground beef or lamb
- 1 onion, chopped
- 2 garlic cloves, minced
- 1 can (14 oz) crushed tomatoes
- 1 tsp cumin
- 1/2 tsp cinnamon
- Salt and pepper
- 2 cups béchamel sauce (milk, butter, flour, and nutmeg)

Instructions:

1. Salt eggplant slices and let them sit for 30 minutes to draw out excess moisture. Pat dry.
2. Sauté onions and garlic, then add ground meat and brown.
3. Add crushed tomatoes, cumin, cinnamon, salt, and pepper. Simmer for 20 minutes.
4. In a separate pan, fry eggplant slices until golden brown.
5. Layer eggplant, meat mixture, and béchamel sauce in a baking dish. Bake at 350°F for 30 minutes.

Baba Ganoush (Eggplant Dip)

Ingredients:

- 2 large eggplants
- 2 cloves garlic, minced
- 1/4 cup tahini
- Juice of 1 lemon
- 2 tbsp olive oil
- Salt and pepper
- Fresh parsley, chopped for garnish

Instructions:

1. Roast the eggplants in a hot oven (400°F) for 30–40 minutes until the skin is charred and the flesh is soft.
2. Scoop out the eggplant flesh and place it in a food processor.
3. Add garlic, tahini, lemon juice, olive oil, salt, and pepper. Blend until smooth.
4. Garnish with parsley and a drizzle of olive oil before serving with pita bread.

Egyptian Tabbouleh

Ingredients:

- 1/2 cup bulgur wheat
- 1 cup finely chopped parsley
- 1/2 cup chopped mint leaves
- 2 tomatoes, diced
- 1 cucumber, diced
- 2 tbsp olive oil
- Juice of 1 lemon
- Salt and pepper

Instructions:

1. Soak bulgur wheat in water for 15 minutes, then drain and fluff with a fork.
2. In a bowl, combine the bulgur with parsley, mint, tomatoes, and cucumber.
3. Drizzle with olive oil, lemon juice, and season with salt and pepper.
4. Chill before serving for the best flavor.

Shorbat Adas (Lentil Soup)

Ingredients:

- 1 cup dried red lentils, rinsed
- 1 onion, chopped
- 2 garlic cloves, minced
- 2 carrots, chopped
- 1 tbsp cumin
- 1 tbsp coriander
- 6 cups vegetable broth
- 2 tbsp olive oil
- Salt and pepper
- Lemon wedges (for serving)

Instructions:

1. In a pot, heat olive oil and sauté onion, garlic, and carrots for 5 minutes.
2. Add lentils, cumin, coriander, broth, and bring to a boil.
3. Simmer for 25–30 minutes until lentils are soft.
4. Season with salt and pepper, and serve with lemon wedges.

Mulukhiyah Soup with Chicken

Ingredients:

- 1 lb chicken (preferably thighs)
- 2 tbsp olive oil
- 4 cloves garlic, minced
- 1 onion, chopped
- 1 tbsp ground coriander
- 6 cups chicken broth
- 1/2 lb frozen or fresh molokhia (jute leaves)
- Lemon wedges (for serving)

Instructions:

1. Cook chicken in olive oil until browned, then remove and set aside.
2. In the same pot, sauté garlic and onion. Add coriander and sauté for 1 more minute.
3. Add chicken broth and bring to a simmer. Add molokhia leaves and cook for 10 minutes.
4. Shred the cooked chicken and return it to the pot. Serve with lemon wedges.

Sweets of Basbousa (Semolina Cake)

Ingredients:

- 1 cup semolina
- 1/2 cup sugar
- 1/2 cup yogurt
- 1/4 cup butter, melted
- 1 tsp baking powder
- 1/2 cup coconut flakes (optional)
- 1/4 cup almonds (for garnish)
- 1 cup simple syrup (1 cup water, 1 cup sugar boiled together)

Instructions:

1. Preheat oven to 350°F. Grease a baking dish.
2. Mix semolina, sugar, yogurt, melted butter, baking powder, and coconut flakes into a smooth batter.
3. Pour the batter into the dish and smooth the top. Score the batter into squares and place an almond on each piece.
4. Bake for 30-35 minutes until golden brown.
5. Pour warm syrup over the hot cake and let it soak for 10 minutes before serving.

Konafa (Shredded Phyllo Pastry with Syrup)

Ingredients:

- 1 lb konafa (shredded phyllo dough)
- 1 cup unsalted butter, melted
- 2 cups ricotta cheese or clotted cream (ashta)
- 1 cup sugar
- 1 cup water
- 1 tsp lemon juice
- 1 tsp rosewater (optional)
- Crushed pistachios for garnish

Instructions:

1. Preheat oven to 350°F. Grease a round baking pan.
2. Gently separate the shredded phyllo dough and toss it with melted butter. Press half of the dough into the bottom of the pan.
3. Spread ricotta cheese or clotted cream evenly over the dough. Cover with the remaining dough and press down firmly.
4. Bake for 25–30 minutes until golden brown and crispy.
5. In a saucepan, combine sugar, water, lemon juice, and rosewater. Bring to a boil, then simmer for 10 minutes to create syrup.
6. Pour hot syrup over the baked konafa and garnish with crushed pistachios.

Sahlab (Egyptian Orchid Drink)

Ingredients:

- 2 tbsp sahlab powder (available in Middle Eastern stores)
- 2 cups milk
- 2 tbsp sugar (adjust to taste)
- 1 tsp ground cinnamon
- 1 tbsp crushed pistachios (for garnish)
- Shredded coconut (optional for garnish)

Instructions:

1. In a pot, heat the milk over medium heat.
2. In a small bowl, mix sahlab powder with a little cold milk to create a smooth paste.
3. Slowly add the paste to the hot milk while stirring constantly.
4. Stir in sugar and cook until the mixture thickens to a creamy consistency (about 5-7 minutes).
5. Pour into cups and garnish with cinnamon, crushed pistachios, and shredded coconut.

Samak Mashwi (Grilled Fish)

Ingredients:

- 2 whole fish (e.g., tilapia or bass), cleaned and gutted
- 3 cloves garlic, minced
- 1 lemon, sliced
- 1 tbsp ground cumin
- 1 tbsp ground coriander
- 1 tbsp paprika
- Salt and pepper to taste
- 2 tbsp olive oil
- Fresh parsley for garnish

Instructions:

1. Preheat the grill or oven to medium heat.
2. In a bowl, combine garlic, cumin, coriander, paprika, olive oil, salt, and pepper.
3. Rub the fish inside and out with the spice mixture.
4. Stuff the fish with lemon slices and fresh parsley.
5. Grill the fish for 10–15 minutes on each side, until the fish is cooked through and the skin is crispy.
6. Garnish with extra parsley before serving.

Kebab Hala (Grilled Lamb Kebabs)

Ingredients:

- 1 lb lamb (cut into cubes)
- 1 onion, grated
- 2 garlic cloves, minced
- 1 tbsp ground cumin
- 1 tbsp ground coriander
- 1 tsp cinnamon
- 1 tbsp fresh mint, chopped
- Salt and pepper to taste
- 2 tbsp olive oil
- Skewers

Instructions:

1. In a bowl, combine lamb cubes, grated onion, garlic, cumin, coriander, cinnamon, mint, olive oil, salt, and pepper.
2. Mix well and let marinate for at least 1 hour in the fridge.
3. Thread lamb cubes onto skewers.
4. Grill over medium heat for 5-7 minutes on each side until cooked to your desired level.
5. Serve with rice or flatbread.

Dukkah (Spice and Nut Mix)

Ingredients:

- 1/4 cup sesame seeds
- 1/4 cup coriander seeds
- 1/4 cup cumin seeds
- 1/4 cup hazelnuts or almonds, chopped
- 1 tbsp ground black pepper
- Salt to taste

Instructions:

1. Toast sesame seeds, coriander seeds, and cumin seeds in a dry skillet over medium heat until fragrant (5-7 minutes).
2. Add the nuts and toast them for another 2 minutes.
3. Let the mixture cool slightly before grinding it in a mortar and pestle or food processor.
4. Add black pepper and salt, and pulse until you get a coarse texture.
5. Serve with bread and olive oil as a dip.

Eish Baladi (Egyptian Flatbread)

Ingredients:

- 3 cups whole wheat flour
- 1 cup all-purpose flour
- 1 tbsp sugar
- 1 tsp salt
- 1 tbsp instant yeast
- 1 1/2 cups warm water
- 2 tbsp olive oil

Instructions:

1. In a large bowl, combine the whole wheat flour, all-purpose flour, sugar, salt, and yeast.
2. Gradually add warm water and olive oil, mixing to form a dough.
3. Knead for 10 minutes until smooth, then cover and let it rise for 1 hour.
4. Preheat a griddle or baking stone.
5. Divide the dough into small balls and roll them into flat circles.
6. Cook each flatbread on the griddle for about 2–3 minutes per side, until slightly puffed and golden.

Sayadeya (Fish Pilaf)

Ingredients:

- 1 lb white fish (e.g., cod or tilapia), filleted
- 1 1/2 cups rice, rinsed
- 1 onion, chopped
- 2 garlic cloves, minced
- 1 tsp ground cumin
- 1/2 tsp cinnamon
- 2 tbsp olive oil
- 2 cups fish stock or water
- 1 tbsp lemon juice
- Salt and pepper to taste

Instructions:

1. In a pan, heat olive oil and sauté onions and garlic until softened.
2. Add cumin, cinnamon, and salt, and cook for 1 minute.
3. Stir in rice and toast it for 2 minutes.
4. Add fish stock or water, bring to a simmer, then cover and cook for 15 minutes.
5. Add the fish fillets on top of the rice and cook for another 10 minutes, until the fish is cooked through.
6. Drizzle with lemon juice before serving.

Kebda Eskandarani (Alexandrian-style Liver)

Ingredients:

- 1 lb beef liver, sliced
- 2 tbsp olive oil
- 1 onion, chopped
- 3 garlic cloves, minced
- 1-2 hot green chilies, chopped
- 1 tsp cumin
- 1/2 tsp ground coriander
- 1/2 tsp ground turmeric
- 1 tbsp vinegar
- Salt and pepper to taste
- Fresh parsley for garnish

Instructions:

1. Heat olive oil in a pan and sauté onions and garlic until soft.
2. Add chilies, cumin, coriander, and turmeric, and cook for 2 minutes.
3. Add liver slices, salt, and pepper, and cook until browned (about 5-7 minutes).
4. Drizzle with vinegar, stir, and cook for another 2 minutes.
5. Garnish with fresh parsley and serve with rice or bread.

Warak Enab (Stuffed Grape Leaves)

Ingredients:

- 1 jar grape leaves (about 30 leaves), drained and rinsed
- 1 cup rice, rinsed
- 1 onion, finely chopped
- 1/4 cup pine nuts
- 1/4 cup olive oil
- 1 tsp ground cinnamon
- 1 tsp allspice
- 1 tbsp lemon juice
- Salt and pepper to taste

Instructions:

1. In a pan, heat olive oil and sauté onions until soft.
2. Add pine nuts, rice, cinnamon, allspice, salt, and pepper. Stir to combine, then add 1 cup of water and cook the rice halfway through.
3. Stuff grape leaves with a small amount of the rice mixture, folding the sides in and rolling tightly.
4. Place the stuffed grape leaves in a pot, layering them as you go.
5. Pour lemon juice and water over the top, cover, and simmer for 40 minutes.

Shakshuka (Poached Eggs in Tomato Sauce)

Ingredients:

- 2 tbsp olive oil
- 1 onion, chopped
- 1 bell pepper, chopped
- 3 garlic cloves, minced
- 1 tsp ground cumin
- 1 tsp ground paprika
- 1/4 tsp ground cayenne pepper (optional)
- 1 can (400g) diced tomatoes
- Salt and pepper to taste
- 4 large eggs
- Fresh parsley or cilantro, chopped (for garnish)

Instructions:

1. Heat olive oil in a large skillet over medium heat. Add the onion and bell pepper, and cook for 5-7 minutes until softened.

2. Add the garlic, cumin, paprika, and cayenne (if using), and cook for 1 minute until fragrant.

3. Add the diced tomatoes with their juice, season with salt and pepper, and simmer for 10 minutes until the sauce thickens.

4. Make four small wells in the sauce and crack the eggs into each well.

5. Cover and cook for 5-7 minutes, or until the eggs are cooked to your desired level.

6. Garnish with fresh parsley or cilantro and serve with warm pita bread.

Sabich (Eggplant and Egg Sandwich)

Ingredients:

- 2 medium eggplants, sliced into 1/2-inch rounds
- Olive oil for frying
- 4 hard-boiled eggs, peeled and sliced
- 4 pita breads
- 1 cup hummus
- 1/2 cup Israeli salad (tomato, cucumber, onion, and parsley)
- 1/4 cup tahini sauce
- 1/4 cup pickled vegetables (optional)
- Salt and pepper to taste

Instructions:

1. Heat olive oil in a frying pan over medium heat. Fry the eggplant slices in batches until golden and tender, about 3-4 minutes per side. Remove and drain on paper towels.
2. Toast the pita breads lightly, then cut them open to form pockets.
3. Spread a layer of hummus inside each pita pocket.
4. Stuff the pita with fried eggplant slices, hard-boiled eggs, Israeli salad, pickled vegetables (if using), and a drizzle of tahini sauce.
5. Season with salt and pepper and serve immediately.

Chicken Mahshi (Stuffed Chicken)

Ingredients:

- 1 whole chicken, cleaned and patted dry
- 1 cup rice, rinsed
- 1 onion, chopped
- 1/4 cup pine nuts
- 1/4 cup currants or raisins
- 1 tbsp ground cinnamon
- 1 tbsp ground cumin
- Salt and pepper to taste
- 2 tbsp olive oil
- 4 cups chicken broth
- 2 tbsp butter

Instructions:

1. Preheat your oven to 375°F (190°C).
2. In a pan, heat olive oil over medium heat and sauté the chopped onion until softened. Add pine nuts and currants, and cook for an additional 2 minutes.
3. Add the rice, cinnamon, cumin, salt, and pepper, and stir to combine. Cook for 5 minutes, then remove from heat and let cool slightly.
4. Stuff the chicken with the rice mixture, then sew or tie the chicken closed.

5. Place the chicken in a roasting pan, pour chicken broth around it, and dot the chicken with butter.

6. Roast for 1.5 to 2 hours, basting occasionally, until the chicken is golden brown and fully cooked. Serve with a side of the rice and vegetables.

Shawarma Spiced Fries

Ingredients:

- 4 large russet potatoes, cut into fries
- 2 tbsp olive oil
- 1 tbsp ground cumin
- 1 tbsp ground paprika
- 1 tsp ground coriander
- 1/2 tsp garlic powder
- 1/2 tsp ground turmeric
- Salt and pepper to taste
- Fresh parsley for garnish

Instructions:

1. Preheat your oven to 400°F (200°C).
2. Toss the cut potatoes in olive oil, shawarma spices, salt, and pepper.
3. Spread the fries evenly on a baking sheet and bake for 25-30 minutes, flipping halfway through, until golden and crispy.
4. Garnish with fresh parsley and serve as a side dish or with tahini sauce for dipping.

Batata Harra (Spicy Potatoes)

Ingredients:

- 4 large potatoes, peeled and diced
- 3 tbsp olive oil
- 3 garlic cloves, minced
- 1-2 red chilies, chopped (optional)
- 1 tsp ground cumin
- 1 tsp paprika
- Salt and pepper to taste
- Fresh cilantro for garnish

Instructions:

1. Heat olive oil in a large skillet over medium heat. Add diced potatoes and cook, turning occasionally, until golden and crispy, about 15-20 minutes.
2. Add the garlic, red chilies, cumin, paprika, salt, and pepper, and cook for another 3-4 minutes until fragrant.
3. Remove from heat and garnish with fresh cilantro. Serve as a side dish or snack.

Egyptian Koshari with Meat

Ingredients:

- 1 cup rice, rinsed
- 1/2 cup lentils
- 1/2 cup elbow macaroni
- 1 onion, chopped
- 1 garlic clove, minced
- 1 lb ground beef or lamb
- 1 can (400g) diced tomatoes
- 1 tbsp ground cumin
- 1 tbsp ground coriander
- 1/2 tsp ground cinnamon
- Salt and pepper to taste
- Fried onions for garnish (optional)

Instructions:

1. Cook the lentils in a pot of boiling water for 15-20 minutes, until tender. Drain and set aside.
2. Cook the rice in a separate pot according to package instructions.
3. Cook the macaroni and drain.
4. In a pan, sauté the onion and garlic until soft. Add the ground meat and cook until browned. Stir in the diced tomatoes, cumin, coriander, cinnamon, salt, and

pepper, and simmer for 10 minutes.

5. To serve, layer the rice, lentils, and macaroni on a plate. Top with the meat mixture and garnish with fried onions if desired.

Tamarind Drink (Amr El-Din)

Ingredients:

- 1/4 cup tamarind paste
- 4 cups water
- 1/2 cup sugar (or to taste)
- Ice cubes (optional)

Instructions:

1. In a pot, combine tamarind paste and water, stirring to dissolve the paste.
2. Bring the mixture to a boil, then reduce heat and simmer for 5-10 minutes.
3. Add sugar to taste and stir until dissolved.
4. Let it cool before serving. Serve chilled with ice cubes if desired.

Qatayef (Stuffed Pancakes)

Ingredients:

- 1 cup all-purpose flour
- 1/2 cup semolina flour
- 1 tsp active dry yeast
- 1 tbsp sugar
- 1/2 tsp baking powder
- 1/2 tsp salt
- 1 cup warm water
- 1/2 cup unsalted ricotta cheese (or sweetened cream cheese)
- 1/4 cup walnuts or pistachios, chopped
- 1 tbsp sugar
- Honey or syrup for drizzling

Instructions:

1. In a bowl, combine the flours, yeast, sugar, baking powder, and salt. Gradually add warm water and mix until smooth. Let the batter rest for 30 minutes to rise.

2. Heat a non-stick pan over medium heat and pour in small circles of batter. Cook for 1-2 minutes, or until bubbles form on the surface, then remove from heat (do not flip).

3. In a separate bowl, mix the ricotta, chopped nuts, and sugar.

4. Place a spoonful of the filling onto the center of each pancake. Fold the pancake over and pinch the edges to seal.

5. Fry the stuffed qatayef in hot oil until golden, then drizzle with honey or syrup before serving.

Shamsiya (Fried Pastry with Honey)

Ingredients:

- 1 1/2 cups all-purpose flour
- 1/2 tsp salt
- 1/2 tsp active dry yeast
- 1/2 cup warm water
- 1 tbsp olive oil
- Oil for frying
- 1/4 cup honey
- 1 tbsp rose water (optional)
- Powdered sugar for dusting (optional)

Instructions:

1. In a bowl, combine the flour, salt, and yeast. Gradually add warm water and olive oil, mixing until a dough forms.
2. Knead the dough for 10 minutes, then cover and let it rise for 1 hour, or until doubled in size.
3. Roll the dough into small balls, then flatten each one into a small circle.
4. Heat oil in a deep pan or fryer to 350°F (175°C). Fry the dough circles until golden brown and crispy, about 2-3 minutes.
5. Drain the pastries on paper towels and set aside.

6. In a small pan, heat the honey with the rose water (if using) until warm. Drizzle the honey over the fried pastries.

7. Dust with powdered sugar if desired and serve warm.

Molokhia with Rabbit

Ingredients:

- 1 rabbit, cut into pieces
- 1 onion, chopped
- 4 cloves garlic, minced
- 1 tbsp ground coriander
- 1/2 tsp ground cumin
- 1/2 tsp turmeric
- 1/2 tsp black pepper
- Salt to taste
- 1 1/2 lbs frozen molokhia (jute leaves) or fresh if available
- 6 cups chicken or rabbit broth
- 2 tbsp olive oil
- 1 tbsp butter
- 1 tbsp lemon juice
- 2 tbsp vinegar
- Rice, for serving (optional)

Instructions:

1. In a large pot, heat olive oil over medium heat. Brown the rabbit pieces on all sides, then remove and set aside.

2. In the same pot, sauté the onion and garlic until fragrant and soft.

3. Add the coriander, cumin, turmeric, black pepper, and salt. Stir for 1 minute until the spices are fragrant.

4. Add the rabbit back into the pot, then pour in the broth. Bring to a boil, then reduce heat and simmer for 1 hour until the rabbit is tender.

5. Once the rabbit is cooked, remove it and set aside. Add the molokhia to the pot and cook for 5 minutes, stirring occasionally.

6. Add the lemon juice, vinegar, and butter to the molokhia. Stir to combine.

7. Serve the molokhia with rice, if desired, and garnish with the rabbit pieces on top.

Bamia (Okra Stew)

Ingredients:

- 1 lb fresh or frozen okra, trimmed
- 1 lb beef or lamb stew meat, cubed
- 1 onion, chopped
- 2 cloves garlic, minced
- 2 tbsp olive oil
- 1 can (400g) diced tomatoes
- 1 tbsp ground coriander
- 1 tsp ground cumin
- Salt and pepper to taste
- 4 cups beef or vegetable broth
- 1 tbsp lemon juice

Instructions:

1. In a large pot, heat olive oil over medium heat. Brown the meat cubes on all sides, then remove and set aside.

2. In the same pot, sauté the onion and garlic until soft and fragrant.

3. Add the tomatoes, coriander, cumin, salt, and pepper, and cook for 5 minutes.

4. Add the browned meat back into the pot along with the broth. Bring to a boil, then reduce heat and simmer for 45 minutes until the meat is tender.

5. Add the okra and lemon juice, and cook for another 20 minutes until the okra is tender.

6. Serve hot with rice or pita bread.

Hummus Bi Tahini (Chickpea Dip)

Ingredients:

- 1 can (400g) chickpeas, drained and rinsed
- 1/4 cup tahini
- 2 tbsp lemon juice
- 2 tbsp olive oil
- 2 garlic cloves, minced
- Salt to taste
- Water as needed
- Paprika and olive oil for garnish

Instructions:

1. In a food processor, combine chickpeas, tahini, lemon juice, olive oil, garlic, and salt.
2. Blend until smooth, adding water gradually to reach your desired consistency.
3. Transfer to a serving bowl and drizzle with olive oil. Garnish with paprika.
4. Serve with pita bread, vegetables, or crackers.

Lentil and Rice Salad with Lemon Dressing

Ingredients:

- 1 cup cooked lentils
- 1 cup cooked rice (preferably brown rice)
- 1/2 cup chopped cucumber
- 1/2 cup chopped red onion
- 1/4 cup chopped parsley
- 1/4 cup olive oil
- 2 tbsp lemon juice
- 1 tbsp Dijon mustard
- Salt and pepper to taste

Instructions:

1. In a large bowl, combine cooked lentils, rice, cucumber, red onion, and parsley.
2. In a separate small bowl, whisk together olive oil, lemon juice, Dijon mustard, salt, and pepper to make the dressing.
3. Pour the dressing over the salad and toss to combine.
4. Chill for 30 minutes before serving to allow the flavors to meld.

Tzatziki-style Yogurt with Garlic and Cucumber

Ingredients:

- 1 cup Greek yogurt
- 1/2 cucumber, grated and drained
- 2 garlic cloves, minced
- 1 tbsp lemon juice
- 1 tbsp olive oil
- Salt and pepper to taste
- Fresh dill for garnish

Instructions:

1. In a bowl, combine Greek yogurt, grated cucumber, garlic, lemon juice, olive oil, salt, and pepper.
2. Stir until smooth and well combined.
3. Garnish with fresh dill and serve chilled with pita or vegetables.

Nile Perch with Tahini Sauce

Ingredients:

- 4 Nile perch fillets (or any white fish fillets)
- 2 tbsp olive oil
- Salt and pepper to taste
- 1/4 cup tahini
- 2 tbsp lemon juice
- 1 garlic clove, minced
- 2 tbsp water (to thin the sauce)
- Fresh parsley for garnish

Instructions:

1. Preheat the grill or a skillet over medium heat. Season the Nile perch fillets with olive oil, salt, and pepper.
2. Grill or cook the fish for 4-5 minutes per side, until cooked through and flaky.
3. In a small bowl, whisk together tahini, lemon juice, garlic, and water to make the sauce.
4. Drizzle the tahini sauce over the grilled fish and garnish with fresh parsley.
5. Serve with rice or a side of vegetables.

Sweet Potato and Honey Fritters

Ingredients:

- 2 large sweet potatoes, peeled and grated
- 1/4 cup flour
- 1/4 tsp ground cinnamon
- 1/4 tsp ground nutmeg
- 1 egg, beaten
- 2 tbsp honey
- Oil for frying

Instructions:

1. In a large bowl, combine grated sweet potatoes, flour, cinnamon, nutmeg, egg, and honey.
2. Heat oil in a pan over medium heat. Spoon the sweet potato mixture into the pan and flatten slightly to form fritters.
3. Fry for 3-4 minutes per side, until golden and crispy.
4. Drain on paper towels and serve with extra honey drizzled on top.

Mashed Fava Beans (Ful Medames)

Ingredients:

- 2 cups dried fava beans (or 2 cans of fava beans)
- 3 cloves garlic, minced
- 1/4 cup olive oil
- 1 tbsp lemon juice
- 1/2 tsp ground cumin
- Salt and pepper to taste
- Chopped parsley (optional)
- Chopped tomatoes (optional)
- Pita bread for serving

Instructions:

1. If using dried fava beans, soak them overnight in water. Drain and cook in a pot of water for 1-1.5 hours, or until tender. If using canned fava beans, drain and rinse them.
2. In a large pan, heat olive oil and sauté the garlic for 2-3 minutes until fragrant.
3. Add the cooked fava beans to the pan, and mash them with a potato masher or fork until smooth.
4. Stir in lemon juice, cumin, salt, and pepper. Cook for 5-7 minutes until heated through.
5. Garnish with parsley and tomatoes, if desired, and serve with pita bread.

Egyptian Falafel Sandwich (Taameya)

Ingredients:

- 2 cups dried fava beans, soaked overnight
- 1/2 onion, chopped
- 3 cloves garlic, minced
- 1/4 cup fresh parsley
- 1/4 cup fresh cilantro
- 1 tsp ground cumin
- 1 tsp ground coriander
- 1/2 tsp baking soda
- Salt and pepper to taste
- Vegetable oil for frying
- Pita bread for serving
- Toppings: lettuce, tomatoes, pickles, tahini sauce

Instructions:

1. Drain and rinse the soaked fava beans. In a food processor, combine the beans, onion, garlic, parsley, cilantro, cumin, coriander, baking soda, salt, and pepper. Pulse until the mixture is finely chopped but not pureed.

2. Transfer the mixture to a bowl, cover, and refrigerate for 1-2 hours to firm up.

3. Heat oil in a deep frying pan over medium heat.

4. Form the falafel mixture into small balls or patties and fry for 3-4 minutes per side until golden brown and crispy.

5. Drain on paper towels and serve in pita bread with lettuce, tomatoes, pickles, and a drizzle of tahini sauce.

Eish Meshmesh (Peach Bread)

Ingredients:

- 2 cups all-purpose flour
- 1/2 cup sugar
- 1/2 cup yogurt
- 1/4 cup olive oil
- 2 eggs
- 2 peaches, peeled and chopped
- 1 tsp baking powder
- 1/2 tsp baking soda
- 1/2 tsp ground cinnamon
- Pinch of salt
- Powdered sugar for dusting (optional)

Instructions:

1. Preheat the oven to 350°F (175°C). Grease a loaf pan with oil or butter.
2. In a large bowl, mix the flour, sugar, baking powder, baking soda, cinnamon, and salt.
3. In a separate bowl, whisk together the eggs, yogurt, and olive oil.
4. Fold the wet ingredients into the dry ingredients until just combined. Gently stir in the chopped peaches.

5. Pour the batter into the prepared loaf pan and bake for 40-45 minutes, or until a toothpick inserted comes out clean.

6. Let the bread cool in the pan for 10 minutes, then transfer to a wire rack. Dust with powdered sugar before serving, if desired.

Beid Bel Daqa (Eggs with Spices)

Ingredients:

- 6 eggs
- 2 tbsp olive oil
- 1 onion, chopped
- 2 tomatoes, chopped
- 1 tsp ground cumin
- 1/2 tsp ground coriander
- 1/2 tsp ground turmeric
- 1/2 tsp paprika
- Salt and pepper to taste
- Fresh parsley for garnish

Instructions:

1. In a skillet, heat olive oil over medium heat. Add the chopped onion and sauté until soft and golden, about 5 minutes.
2. Add the chopped tomatoes and cook for 5 more minutes until they soften.
3. Stir in the cumin, coriander, turmeric, paprika, salt, and pepper.
4. Crack the eggs directly into the skillet and cook until the whites are set, but the yolks are still soft, about 4-5 minutes.
5. Garnish with fresh parsley and serve with pita bread.

Sogok (Honeyed Pistachio Dessert)

Ingredients:

- 1 cup shelled pistachios, chopped
- 1/4 cup sugar
- 2 tbsp honey
- 1 tbsp butter
- 1/2 tsp ground cinnamon
- 1/4 tsp ground cardamom

Instructions:

1. In a small pan, melt the butter over low heat. Add the pistachios, sugar, honey, cinnamon, and cardamom.
2. Stir until the pistachios are well coated and the sugar dissolves, about 5 minutes.
3. Remove from heat and let the mixture cool to room temperature.
4. Serve the pistachio mixture as a dessert or snack.

Al-Mahshi Kousa (Stuffed Zucchini)

Ingredients:

- 6 medium zucchini, hollowed out
- 1 lb ground beef or lamb
- 1 onion, chopped
- 1/2 cup rice, rinsed
- 1/4 cup parsley, chopped
- 1 tsp ground cumin
- 1/2 tsp ground cinnamon
- Salt and pepper to taste
- 2 cups tomato sauce
- 1 tbsp olive oil

Instructions:

1. In a skillet, sauté the chopped onion in olive oil until soft. Add the ground meat and cook until browned.

2. Stir in the rice, parsley, cumin, cinnamon, salt, and pepper. Cook for 2-3 minutes to combine.

3. Stuff the zucchini with the meat and rice mixture, making sure they are tightly packed.

4. Place the stuffed zucchinis in a large pot and pour the tomato sauce over them. Add enough water to cover the zucchini.

5. Cover the pot, bring to a simmer, and cook for 45-60 minutes until the zucchini is tender and the rice is cooked through.

Smoked Salmon with Tahini

Ingredients:

- 8 oz smoked salmon
- 2 tbsp tahini
- 1 tbsp lemon juice
- 1 tbsp olive oil
- Salt and pepper to taste
- Fresh dill for garnish

Instructions:

1. In a small bowl, whisk together tahini, lemon juice, olive oil, salt, and pepper to make the sauce.
2. Plate the smoked salmon and drizzle the tahini sauce over the top.
3. Garnish with fresh dill and serve with pita bread or crackers.

Hawaij (Spiced Rice)

Ingredients:

- 2 cups basmati rice
- 1 tbsp olive oil
- 1 onion, chopped
- 1 tsp ground cumin
- 1/2 tsp ground coriander
- 1/2 tsp ground turmeric
- Salt to taste
- 4 cups chicken or vegetable broth

Instructions:

1. Rinse the rice under cold water until the water runs clear.
2. In a large pot, heat olive oil over medium heat. Add the chopped onion and sauté until soft.
3. Stir in the cumin, coriander, turmeric, and salt. Cook for 1 minute.
4. Add the rice to the pot and stir to coat with the spices.
5. Add the broth and bring to a boil. Reduce the heat, cover, and simmer for 15-20 minutes, or until the rice is tender and the liquid is absorbed.

Egyptian Pudding with Cinnamon (Om Ali)

Ingredients:

- 1 package puff pastry, thawed and cut into small pieces
- 2 cups whole milk
- 1/4 cup sugar
- 1/4 tsp ground cinnamon
- 1/2 cup chopped nuts (such as almonds, pistachios, or walnuts)
- 1/2 cup raisins
- 1/2 cup coconut flakes

Instructions:

1. Preheat the oven to 350°F (175°C). Place the puff pastry pieces in a baking dish and bake for 10-15 minutes until golden brown.
2. In a saucepan, heat the milk, sugar, and cinnamon over medium heat until it begins to simmer. Stir occasionally.
3. Add the baked puff pastry pieces to the milk mixture and stir in the chopped nuts, raisins, and coconut flakes.
4. Pour the mixture into a baking dish and bake for 20-25 minutes, or until the top is golden and the pudding is set.
5. Serve warm with a drizzle of honey if desired.

www.ingramcontent.com/pod-product-compliance
Lightning Source LLC
LaVergne TN
LVHW081318060526
838201LV00055B/2354